Tommaso

Handbook of
Active
Meditation

Peaceflow in action

Contents

Introduction

I have been seeing people suffering from stress and anxiety for more than twenty years and, during the course of the first nine years, I have employed different approaches to help them overcome their problem: from hypnosis to Jungian analysis, and from humanistic counselling to cognitive-behavioural therapies (i.e. CBT, REBT, Multimodal Therapy).

The application of the above models did not allow me to embrace the whole person though. It was easy to identify archetypes, symptoms, thought patterns and behaviours, but I could as easily lose touch with the real persons sitting in front of me!

To remedy that, in January 2000, I created Open CBT, a new integrative approach whose practical application consists of a 15-step person care process that addresses the three components which make up each human being (physical sensations, emotions and thoughts).

Addressing my clients' problems by adopting the above approach has given me considerable professional satisfaction. However, in the summer of 2005 I felt that there still was something missing: my model was *only* a talking cure and I was not working with people's bodies.

I have always believed that human beings are a unity of mindbodyspirit and have personally experienced the benefits of practices like yoga, tai chi, and shiatsu.

It was comforting to read how world-famous psychiatrists, who were (and still are) leading experts in their field, like David Servan-Schreiber and Bessel van der Kolk, had started writing openly about the value and usefulness of bodywork.

As Servan-Schreiber observed: *"Neuroscience research has shown clearly that the basic disorders involving depression, stress and anxiety are all related to the functioning of our emotional brain, which we mostly do not understand and look after badly. The same research explains why concentrating on the body can be so effective. Besides producing emotions, the limbic system is also intimately linked with our major metabolic systems – the heart, the guts, the hormones and the immune system. There is constant two-way traffic, with messages coming up about what is going on in the body and messages going out to ensure a smooth working of the whole...This new picture explains why working with the body can be more effective than psychotherapeutic talking cures – the links between the emotional brain and the body are denser and faster than those between the emotional brain and the cortex."* (1)

Bessel van der Kolk also noted how:
"The imprint of trauma is the imprint on people's senses, on people's sensory systems. That becomes particularly important because these

sensations stay in people's memory banks and stay unprocessed. If you do effective trauma processing, the individual smells, sounds, images and physical impressions of the trauma slowly disappear over time and that is something that doesn't happen with talking. It happens by working with people's bodily states. When a person experiences trauma, they become highly aroused and, for a period of time, lose their capacity for self-regulation. Parts of the frontal lobe that deal with the capacity to plan, to rationalise, to inhibit inappropriate behaviour – and specifically one area associated with speech – are shown to shut down. People who have experienced trauma need to feel safe in their bodies again. It's via the awareness of deep bodily experience that people

11

can begin to move around the way they feel." (2)

At that point my new challenge became the integration of my person care programme with a suitable bodywork practice.

I reviewed all the main bodywork practices being applied at that time and found them all interesting and stimulating. However, they were either too rigid or too floppy, and none of them was providing an integration between gentle body movement and psychological work.

It was then that I decided to create a new active meditation practice which would address the whole person by including in the same routine meditation, visualisation, bodywork & psychological techniques.

This is how Peaceflow, my active meditation routine, comes about. Since May 2005, I have taught Peaceflow to people suffering from stress, anxiety and sleep problems.

The time has now come to take Peaceflow beyond the boundaries of my consulting room and share it with all those who can benefit from its regular practice.

Tommaso Palumbo
London, 4 March 2017

Chapter 1
Energy

*"The more fully we give our energy,
the more it returns to us."*

Buddha (1)

What is Peaceflow?

With words we may say everything, but our body never lies.

Peaceflow is a form of active meditation which consists of a warm-up routine and seven movements specifically designed to help us unwind and reconnect with the Life forces within.

We are already aware of the benefits of meditation and of including a regular exercise routine in our life. But there are other good reasons to make more use of our body.

When we exercise – as well as when we engage in creative activities or when we dream – we activate the right hemisphere of our brain and this allows a beneficial discharge of the excess energy which we tend to accumulate in the left hemisphere during the day.

Focusing on our body also helps us switch off those worries and negative thoughts that we constantly build up in the left hemisphere, and the UK National Institute for Clinical Excellence has confirmed the use of exercise as a primary treatment for mild to moderate depression. (2)

However, when we feel down and depressed, we tend to reduce considerably our movements and withdraw from social contacts.

In such cases, going to the gym or simply going out may feel too much like hard work.

Reconnecting with our body, through gentle bodywork and touch, can help us reverse this downward spiral gradually and comfortably.

There is no such thing as different 'selves' inhabiting our body: a human being is a unity of mind, body and spirit: different components or elements are only the diverse facets by which we perceive who we are.

Movement is change of energy, and this is what we are looking for when we experience stress, anxiety and sleep problems.

By 'change' we do not mean that there is necessarily something wrong with us: to the contrary, we acknowledge that we are perfectly functioning integrated systems, which would, most of the time, only benefit from assuming a different 'position' towards ourselves and our physical and social environment.

Research carried out at the Royal Hallamshire Hospital in Sheffield (UK), the US National Institute of Health and Harvard's Women's

Health Watch on the regular practice of Tai chi, have already shown that gentle bodywork slows the heart rate and lowers blood pressure in heart attack victims.

Moreover, it is effective against arthritis, bone loss and ageing and has a positive effect on diabetes, lower back pain and depression.

Peaceflow, is a style of active meditation, which is different from traditional forms of gym exercises, or practices like Tai chi, because:

- it is easy to learn;

- its movements are easy to remember;

- everybody can practise it, regardless of their age, shape and how fit they are;

- movements are not set in stone but allow for personal variations;

- it is relaxing and pleasurable, unlike the stressful efforts so often associated with gym exercises;

- it frees us from the *curse of the mirror*, that is we can forget about how we look and focus purely on our wellbeing;

- Peaceflow also provides simple psychological tools which are beautifully integrated into its gentle body movements.

Why Peaceflow?

As physical movement enhances a person's capacity for movement of thought, so the awareness of our flow of energy can help us reconnect with our inner vital resources, which originate from our bond with the natural world.

What do we mean by "energy"? We are certainly not referring to some sort of ethereal and mysterious entity, dreamed by an ascetic master thousands of years ago: we can feel and touch our internal energy any time we want!

Just place your hand on your wrist, what do you feel? The sensation of warmth coming from this contact is the result of the vital activity of billions of cells in your body: you are alive thanks to their energy, which is yours to dispose of.

Recent research has shown how each human cell is a wonderful autonomous system on its own, while, at the same time, being perfectly integrated with its environment, that is, our entire body.

Energy flows through our body thanks to the blood circulation, the lymphatic system and nerve endings which play the fundamental role of connecting each square millimetre of our body.

Traditional Chinese medicine has, for thousands of years, focused its attention on how important it is to look after and, possibly enhance, the internal flow of energy throughout our body, in order to prevent and cure a number of illnesses.

Practices now fully recognised in Western societies, such as acupuncture, yoga, shiatsu and tai chi, are all based on the Eastern assumption that illnesses and discomfort arise when the flow of energy is either blocked or in excess in some specific areas of our body.

Centuries of practical work on energy and the experiential awareness acquired have indicated to Eastern practitioners that there are a number of energy lines which cover the full length of our body: they call them meridians.

The correct practice of appropriate movements – like the ones indicated in our Peaceflow steps – result in a free flow of energy that can be greatly beneficial for our well-being.

The main purpose of Peaceflow is to widen your horizon and help you reconnect with the Life forces which are already present, within you (i.e. the power of your breathing, the energy of your heart beating, etc.).

This is a process which asks for first-hand experience of the points being introduced.

The aim of Peaceflow's movement is to show you signposts of how to get to a number of paths, which only you can follow.

Warm up

Internal balance and strength are not qualities inherited from birth. They come from aligning the body, opening the joints and relaxing the muscles.

The Chinese call our vital energy 'Chi' – 'Ki' in Japanese. We will simply refer to it as 'energy'.

The movements of active meditation are specifically designed to help you rebalance the flow of energy through your body.

Therefore, their principal focus is the very centre of energy in your body.

The Chinese call this 'Tan T'ien' and the Japanese 'Hara', and is located approximately 1 and ½ inches below the navel.

From now on, we will call our energy centre simply 'the centre'.

All Peaceflow movements will be more effective if you feel your centre and feel that, with your breathing, you are spreading the flow of energy from your centre to each part of your body.

So, when you breathe in, first make sure that the air reaches your lower abdomen, next visualise that it touches your centre, and then, that it spreads to each part of your body before you breathe out.

The warm-up is made up of three sections:

- Tuning in
- The Wave
- The Circle

Tuning in.

Eastern medicine views the body as a musical instrument, which needs to be tuned to fulfil its potential and generate sound.

Please note that you are required to carry out each movement **very slowly**, **gently** and **gradually**: this will ensure your full enjoyment as well as the beneficial outcome of your practice. Fast, sudden and abrupt movements can cause discomfort or injury, especially if you haven't exercised for some time.

1. Assume the starting position.

   a) stand, as if the head is suspended from the ceiling;

   b) bend the knees slightly to lower the centre of gravity and stretch the spine;

   c) sink the shoulders to release the tension built there;

   d) breathe deep into the abdomen.

Make sure that your knees do not go beyond the imaginary perpendicular line which aligns them with the tips of your toes. Once you are satisfied that your posture is correct, close your eyes and take a few deep breaths.

Breathe slowly, gently and deeply (exactly in this order), in this starting position for a couple of minutes.

2. Bring your knees back to the normal standing posture and then bend them to reassume the starting position a few times. First, breathe in, allowing the air to expand your chest and accompanying this movement with an 'opening up' of your arms and hands. Then, breathe out as you are bending your knees.

3. Breathe in as you gently tilt your body forward, ensuring that your feet are firmly on the floor. Then, breathe out as you tilt your body forward.

4. Breathe in as you tilt your body from left to right. Then, breathe out as you tilt from right the left. Next, do the same in reverse.

5. Breathe in as you move your body in a circular motion clockwise (first half of the circular movement). Then, breathe out when you do the second half of the circular movement. Next, do the same anti-clockwise.

5. Breathe in as your tilt your pelvis forward and breathe out as you tilt it backwards.

6. Breathe in as your tilt your pelvis from left to right. Then, breathe out as you tilt from right the left. Next, do the same in reverse.

7. Breathe in as you move your pelvis/hips in a circular motion clockwise (first half of the circular movement). Then, breathe out when you do the second half of the circular movement. Next, do the same anti-clockwise.

8. Bend your right leg forward, while the left leg goes slightly backward. Make sure that you feel balanced and comfortable. Breathe in as you move your weight forward onto the right leg and your arms go 'fishing' for fresh air in a circular movement. Then, breathe out as your shift your weight backwards and bring your arms to the centre. Next, do the same bending forward the left leg.

9. Raise and extend your arms, gently and slowly, until they are

parallel to the floor. Now, breathe in as our arms move backwards, as if you were taking something in. Then, breathe out as you move your arms forward, as if you were pushing something away, and then return them to your side. Next, do the same but you raise and extend your arms backwards.

10. Breathe in as you keep the starting posture. Then, breathe out as you gently tilt your head down.

11. Breathe in as you gently tilt your head from left to right.Then, breathe out as you tilt from right the left. Next, do the same in reverse.

12. Breathe in as you stretch your body upward, as if you were a puppet on strings and the puppet master

were pulling them up. Then, breathe out as you 'let go' of your body (i.e. head, shoulders, arms, and hands), as if your puppet master were letting go of them.

The wave.

> ➤ Extend your arms, parallel and with palms facing down.

> ➤ Rotate both arms clockwise 90 degrees – that is, your arms are in line with your body with your palms facing left.

> ➤ Move your arms to the left, and then, first, bring your left hand down while the right goes up, and next, with your palms facing right, move your arms to the right.

➢ Bring your right arm down and the left up, with palms facing left, and restart the entire movement again.

It is as if you are drawing a wave with your arms, gently pushing something away, and your body is gently following your arms movements with a slight bending motion of your legs and torso. You breathe in before you start the movement and breathe out as you shift your arms.

The circle.

Stretch both arms to one side and move them in a circular motion, initially, a few times clockwise, then, anticlockwise. It is as if, with your circular movements, you are drawing a circle, which goes from as far as your arms can stretch to your right, to your left and above your head.

Breathe in as you move your arms upwards and breathe out when your arms move downwards.

The seven movements

1. The sailing vessel

➢ Keep your feet firmly rooted to the ground and begin gently undulating your body, initially forward and backward.

- ➢ Then, to the right and to the left.

- ➢ Next, in a circular way, both clockwise and anticlockwise.

- ➢ Finally, carry on by allowing your body to lead you in any direction it may wish to go.

I would suggest you first familiarise yourself with the first two movements, and then, you move to the latter.

This exercise is called the sailing vessel, because, to make the most of it, you would like to imagine that you are a vessel: your feet are the deck and your body is the mast.

Your movements come as a result of sea waves. These waves generate a gentle, slow and powerful rolling that you simply follow with your mast.

You may wish to practise this exercise with your eyes closed: this way you can visualise wonderful coastlines and turquoise seas, swimming dolphins or flying birds, as well as 'feel' a gentle breeze caressing your face.

To complete this exercise, first, make sure that your eyes are closed and assume a true 'mast position', by fully extending your arms: you are now feeling the energy of the sun and the wind, and you are receiving it through your palms.

Next, first extend your arms to the sky, palms facing up, and then, bring both hands to your centre (just below your navel), palms facing in, and keep them there for a few moments.

Finally, slowly open your eyes.

2. The sage's hug

➢ Close your eyes and imagine yourself as a sage. Then, stretch your arms forward, just like you are hugging something or somebody.

➢ Visualise that with your hug you are embracing a wonderful tree, an unknown beautiful woman, or a handsome man, or something or somebody you know. You are receiving a great deal of energy from this embrace.

➢ Stay in that position for 3 to 4 minutes, while continuing to breathe slowly, gently and deeply. Then, relax your arms for a couple of minutes.

➢ Now visualise that you are hugging something or somebody else. This time you are giving them your energy.

➢ At some point, you will feel a tingling in your fingers. When this happens, first extend your arms to the sky, palms facing up, and then, bring both hands to our centre (just below your navel), palms facing in, and

keep them there for a few
moments.

➤ Finally, slowly open your eyes.

With practice, you will be able to
keep your arms stretched for a
longer period of time.

However, as with all our bodywork,
we are not looking for quantity but,
rather, quality: we want to enjoy
Peaceflow movements, from start to
finish – that's our golden rule – and
we complete them when we feel we
are happy to end them.

It is better to carry out our
movements for shorter periods of
time and to enjoy the activity, than to
overdo them and feel discomfort in
the process: what makes a difference

for our wellbeing is regularity of practice, not excessive and episodic efforts!

3. The heron

> ➤ Close your eyes and imagine yourself as a heron in its natural environment: your feet are in the water and the beauty of nature is all around you.

> ➤ Lift your right foot slowly and move it slightly forward with your toes pointing down.

> ➤ Your foot is very close to the ground, but is not touching it.

➢ Then, slowly lift your right knee and stop before your leg reaches the 90 degree angle.

➢ Slowly put your right leg down and do the same with your left.

➢ Next, make a few steps in any direction you like by moving your legs, one by one, according to the above indicated movement: that is, your body weight is first on one leg and then on the other. So, you extend one foot, then lift the leg, and finally, make your step. Then, you do the same with the other leg.

Now, stand with both feet on the ground and your eyes closed.

➢ When you are ready, spread your wings, by lifting your arms, and shake them gently to shed the water.

➢ Feel your wings drying in the warm sun.

To complete this exercise, first extend your arms to the sky, palms facing up, and then, bring both hands to your centre (just below your navel), palms facing in, and keep them there for a few moments.

Finally, slowly open your eyes.

4. The hermit's blessing

➢ Close your eyes and imagine yourself as a hermit who lives on a mountain.

➢ You are standing in the open and you can see a beautiful scenery surrounding you: warm sun, blue sky, mountains, a valley below and a village in the distance.

➢ Become fully aware of the beauty of the nature around you.

➢ Raise your forearms, keeping your elbows by your side, palms facing up – in a thanksgiving posture.

➤ Feel at peace with yourself and nature. Allow the energy of nature to enter your body through your palms and let it spread all over you.

➤ Count the blessings in your life.

➤ Extend – without stretching – your arms forward and direct your palms towards the valley below.

➤ Direct your energy and your blessing toward the valley below and its people.

To complete the exercise, first extend your arms to the sky, palms facing up, and then, bring both hands to your centre (just below your navel), palms facing in, and keep them there for a few moments.

Finally, slowly open your eyes.

5. The dancer

➢ Close your eyes and start a free-flowing dance.

➢ You may visualise that you are dancing on your own or with somebody else.

➢ As you take each step, you want to feel the pleasure of free movement and, at the same time, feel fully balanced.

➢ Next, make a few steps, one leg at a time, as in the heron's exercise.

➢ Now, return to free-flowing movements and make a few joyful steps.

47

To complete the exercise, extend your arms to the sky, palms facing up, like they were antennae receiving the world's energy and converting it into an exhilarating feeling of joy.

Next, guide your hands to a particular place in your body which may benefit from warmth and comfort.

Then, bring both hands to your centre (just below your navel), palms facing in, and keep them there for a few moments.

Finally, slowly open your eyes.

6. The tree

➢ Close your eyes and imagine yourself as a tree.

➢ Feel your centre sinking, first, down to the ground, and then, below the ground, as if you were a tree becoming fully aware of its roots.

➢ Feel the air flowing in and out of your body.

➢ Feel the blood flow.

➢ Feel the energy coming from your roots and let this energy flow all the way up, allowing it to reach the top of your trunk (= your head) and your main branches (= your extended arms).

➢ Now, bring your focus back to your centre and feel your body strong and alive.

➢ Extend your arms slightly and comfortably as if they were tree branches.

➢ Feel that Life is making use of them: birds stop by chirping joyfully and little creatures take refuge from the heat under their shade. You have been there since the beginning of time and you will always be there to provide for the universe's little ones: the ones in search of safety and comfort.

➢ Feel the energy at the very end of your branches (= your hands).

Next, guide your hands to a particular place in your body which may benefit from warmth and comfort.

To complete this exercise, first extend your arms to the sky, palms facing up, and then, bring both hands to your centre (just below your navel), palms facing in, and keep them there for a few moments.

Finally, slowly open your eyes.

7. The eagle's flight

➤ Close your eyes and imagine yourself as an eagle perched on a tree branch.

➤ You are in a beautiful place up in the mountains and the view from your standpoint is breath-taking.

➤ Slowly lift your heels and bring them back to the ground. Do this twice.

➤ Spread your 'wings' and move them as if you were flying away.

➤ Enjoy the stunning view and the wonderful flight by

extending your arms comfortably and making slow and harmonious movements.

➢ Feel light, weightless.

➢ Feel above everything you see. You are so high up nothing can touch you and nobody can reach you.

➢ You breathe the purest air and feel the wind on your face.

➢ Silence is all around: a profound peace possesses you now.

➢ You are flying and your wings are moving, but you are perfectly still within.

➢ Now, find a place where to rest.

➢ Next, guide your hands to a particular place in your body which may benefit from warmth and comfort.

➢ Then, first extend your arms to the sky, palms facing up, and then, bring them down and move both hands to your centre (just below your navel), palms facing in, and keep them there for a few moments.

➢ Finally, slowly open your eyes.

Chapter 2
Presence

The journey within

"Being in control" is what most of you want, in order to be able to manage life's events and pursue your objectives.

However, "being in control" is a condition (or a state of mind, if you wish), which is irreconcilable with the authentic nature of a human being.

We are wonderfully complex, integrated and intelligent systems, but, at the same time, we are limited and fragile.

Therefore, what we would better look for is not "being in control" but "being present to ourselves" – that is, living in a state of awareness.

We cannot control the ever-changing flow of life and life's events, but we can be fully aware of them.

As a result, we can, on the one hand, fully enjoy love and happiness, for the warmth they give to our life; while, on the other, we can fully embrace moments of sadness and distress, for the growing and learning which they bring about.

This is the road which leads to peace and contentment.

I will show you now two techniques which will help you be 'present to yourself': "the seven doors" and "back to life".

The Seven Doors

This practice will ask you to go through seven doors. I would recommend that you go through one door per day. This way, you will be able to memorise the correct sequence of the doors – given that you will be adding just one door at a time, every day, until you reach and go through the seventh – and you will also allow yourself the space to fully explore each room and become aware of your presence there.

Some continue practising by adding one door at a time even when they have memorised the whole sequence: this gives them a sense of self-care, because the seven doors cover each day of the week. Others prefer going through the seven doors every time they practice.

Sit somewhere comfortably, or lay down in bed, if you wish. Close your eyes and slow down your breathing.

When you feel calm and relaxed, begin the practice by following the steps indicated below.

See yourself walking in a beautiful place: it could be a sea resort, somewhere in the country or in the mountains.

At some point, you see a path leading to a house (naturally, the house will reflect the place you are in).

Walk towards the house and reach its main entrance.

Now, you notice that there is a writing on the door (the writing could be engraved, painted or tiled).

The writing on this **first door** says: "**compassion**".

You know that compassion means 'kindness', 'consideration' and 'care', so when you enter the house through the compassion door, you want to visualise a room where you can feel kind, considerate and caring.

The room's layout, furnishing and lighting is entirely up to you, as long as it makes you feel compassionate.

Find a place where you can seat and then first direct the feeling of compassion towards yourself, and then, think of somebody else and direct your feeling of compassion towards him or her.

Once you have allowed enough time to connect with compassion, visualise a second door and make your way towards it.

The writing on the **second door** says: **"emptiness"**.

Here, you would like to create a place where silence reigns: nothing else matters, nothing was, is, or will ever be.

The room's layout, furnishing and lighting is entirely up to you, as long as it makes you feel empty.

Then, take a seat somewhere, find an empty place within you and gradually expand it with each breath you take in and out, until you feel completely empty.

The Roman Emperor and philosopher, Marcus Aurelius, used to say: "If you want to live well, you want to learn to die, every day."

Create emptiness and let yourself go into the sea of nothingness.

As it happens to the seed sown in the earth, that is 'born' and begins its growth in the humid dark of fertile soil, so this room will mother your next step: the rebirth of your inspiration.

The writing on the **third door** says: **"inspiration"**.

Here, you want to feel inspired: the room's layout, furnishing and lighting is entirely up to you, as long as it makes you feel inspired.

Then, find a place where you can seat and think of something or somebody that inspires you.

It could be anything: the sunset, the sea, a mountain's peak, a painting, a writer, a sportsman, a musician or an actor.

Now imagine that you are embracing or touching your source of inspiration and are getting a lot of energy from this contact.

Next, think of somebody you would like to inspire yourself and imagine embracing him or her: this time you are passing on your energy.

Once you have allowed enough time to pass on your energy visualise a fourth door and make your way towards it.

The writing on the **fourth door** says: "**forgiveness**".

You do exactly as you have done in the step before: that is first you create this place, then you take a seat, next you forgive yourself and finally you forgive a person of your choice.

Please note that to forgive does not mean to condone: forgiveness here means letting go of your own suffering, which is a burden you carry around while to condone means to excuse or to reconcile.

You are perfectly entitled to forgive – something or somebody – without having to justify, excuse or reconcile with them.

Forgiving gives you balance and peace, and frees lots of energy, which can be used in more creative or productive ways.

At the same time, forgiving makes of you a more pleasant person to be around.

Once you have allowed enough time to forgive yourself and somebody of your choice, visualise a fifth door and make your way towards it.

The writing on the **fifth door** says: **"peace"**.

You do as you have done before.

Again, feel free to create this place as you wish, then take a seat and first make peace with you, and, only then, make peace with another person of your choice.

Once you have allowed enough time to make peace with yourself and somebody of your choice, visualise a sixth door and make your way towards it.

The writing on the **sixth door** says: "**love**".

As you have done in the 'peace' room, take a seat and begin first by loving yourself, and only then move your feelings of warmth and affection towards somebody else.

Choose a place in your body where you most feel the warmth of love, and gradually expand this wonderful feeling all over your body: allow the transforming and healing power of love into your life, surrendering completely to it.

Once you have allowed enough time to feel love within you, visualise a seventh door and make your way towards it.

The writing on the **seventh door** says: "**happiness**".

As you have done in the 'love' room, take a seat and begin first by feeling happy yourself, and only then think of somebody you would like to share your happiness with.

Next, choose a place in your body where you most feel happy and gradually expand this wonderful feeling all over your body: allow the healing power of happiness into your life, surrendering completely to it.

Once you have allowed enough time to feel happiness within you, you can slowly open your eyes.

Back to Life

Find an appropriate quiet place, at home or at the office. Lower or switch off the light, if you can, and make yourself comfortable.

It would be useful to listen to a recording of your voice reading very slowly the paragraphs below: you could easily do that with a memo or tape recorder, most mobile phones can also perform this function nowadays.

Also, please make sure that you stop for a moment (i.e. 5 to 10 seconds) at the pauses in the text as indicated by the ellipsis symbol '…'.

"Focus your attention on your body. How does it feel? Close your eyes. Take a few slow and deep breaths. Push the air down to your abdomen (= your centre), become aware of your breathing … of the air coming in your body … and of the air going out … feel this flow.

Think of nothing … imagine a sea of emptiness and nothingness … let yourself go into this calm sea of emptiness and nothingness … feel safe and content where you are.

Now, focus on your body … feel your heart beat … listen to it … feel it …

and connect with its flow ... your body keeps you alive ... your lungs breathe ... your heart beats ... the blood flows throughout your body ... billions of nerve cells make you feel cold or warmth ... your body knows what to do ... your body ... in its infinite wisdom ... knows what to do.

Your body is alive ... there are billions of living cells in your body ... there are billions of living cells in a flower ... you are like a flower ... what kind of flower are you? ... what is your colour? ... what is your smell? ... there are billions of cells in a tree ... you are like a tree ... what kind of tree are you? ... what kind of branches do you have? ... little birds are nesting on your tree ... what birds are they? ... what is their colour? ... Feel content and safe where you are.

You are alive ... everything around you is alive ... you are one of billions of living creatures on Earth ... you are filled with Life ... they are filled with Life ... Life is here ... Life is everywhere ... Life is constant change ... Life is flow ... feel the flow of your breath ...

Feel the quiet and silence around you ... take a few deep breaths ... and only when you are ready ... slowly and gently ... open your eyes."

Chapter 3
Light Heart

Open up your heart

Too much thinking poisons our body with goals, worries, deadlines, criticism and assessments.

From time to time, it is very beneficial to disconnect from our rational mind and stop interfering with our inner vital processes.

Switch off the constant noise of your environment and make a bit of time and space to allow silence to embrace you and help you reconnect with Life.

Only when we feel connected with Life, are we able to fully experience the flow of energy that nourishes and supports us and all the living creatures on Earth.

Only then, are we capable of connecting with the sadness and the joy which is within and around us. Only then, can we experience peace.

Thus, opening up our heart is not a specific – though enlightened – action, but rather, a life-long experiential process where we open ourselves up to the depths of our conscience and to the breadth of our world.

One way to do this is to practise the 'connecting with love' technique indicated below.

We are not even attempting here a definition of 'love': we may all have our own ideas of what love is, of how we fall in love or fall out of it. For some love is an everlasting feeling, for others a transient emotion.

In our person care programme, we view love as yet another life force: a powerful and, at times, overwhelming force which can trigger a range of emotional responses, as well as unpredictable choices and behaviours.

Love can change one's life, love has the power to transform who we are and what we do with our life.

We can make a beneficial use of this force by connecting with it and utilising its energy to direct light into our deepest and darkest inner places; to warmly embrace our sadness; to motivate us to break our self-inflicted isolation and grant ourselves permission to go out there and live life.

When you feel low or depressed; when you are not quite sure whether you are in an appropriate place; when you don't feel comfortable with your partner, in particular, or with your social life, in general, you may find it useful to practise the following two techniques: "connecting with love" and "the love pie".

Connecting with love

You will find it easy to remember this exercise because it is divided into four consecutive steps each beginning with the four letters making up the word "love".

You may also wish to listen to your own recording of the steps, as in the "back to Life" technique.

In this case, please allow a pause between each step to ensure you have enough time to carry out the indicated tasks.

Find a quiet place. Switch off your mobile phone and other sources of noise.

Make yourself comfortable and close your eyes. Take a few deep and slow breaths and begin the exercise.

Look inside yourself: go and find your sadness or issue. Find the place in your body where you most feel it.

Observe your sadness or issue. Do not analyse, do not ask questions: just observe it for what and how it is.

Visualise love as light. What is the colour of your love? Find the place in your body where you most feel it.

Experience the warmth that is now, gently and gradually, spreading from the place where you most feel love to the rest of your body.

When you reach the place where you most feel your sadness – or issue – let the light of love go around it, like a warm embrace, until you see and feel that your place of sadness is completely embraced by the light of love.

Let this light penetrate the place of sadness and let it spread within, until this place is completely filled with the light of love.

Observe this. Feel this. Feel the warmth of the light of love, which has now spread all over your body.

Stay there, connected with this feeling, calm and at peace, for a couple of minutes. Then, slowly open your eyes.

The love pie

The following activity may offer you an awareness of your current situation which you might have missed so far, especially if some major unbalance comes up: this may help your motivation in introducing changes in the way you address your personal and social life.

In my professional experience, I have found that people find this activity very stimulating, and often, some interesting points tend to come up.

On day one, begin by writing down the different ways in which somebody – not you in particular – may give and receive love: make one list for giving and one for receiving (your lists may have items like: mother's love, friend's love, etc.).

Once the two lists are completed, number the items in order of how valuable you think they are.

Then, draw a couple of circles (pies), slice them up by inserting the items from your lists, and you may also reflect the value you have attached to your items by drawing a bigger slice for the more valuable items and a smaller slice for the others.

The next day, write down two lists including the different ways in which you are giving and receiving love.

You now proceed as with day one, by placing your items, first, in order of how much you value them, and then, by drawing a couple of pies which will graphically represent your lists.

The third day, you place the two different sets of pies together and observe them: what do they show?

Don't analyse, just observe what you see. Are you a giver or a receiver?

Are you directing your energy mostly towards one or two persons (i.e. your pie shows big slices)? How is the receiving?

Are you happy with what you see or would you like to change something?

The gentle touch

Peaceflow does not only benefit our movement of thought and our flow of energy, it can also help improve our ability to love by removing the blocks that we have placed between us and our personal and social environment.

As Vincenzo Rossi observes: *"If my ability to love is 'ten' and I live only a 'three', out of my potential of ten, given the fundamental unity of mindbodyspirit, my body will only show 30% of all those movements which reflect care, love, affection and joy for life. Therefore, by moving my body beyond that 30%, I evoke a change, at all levels of my being, which will help my personal growth as well as my relating to others." (1)*

Touch can express empathy, care and affection much more than any words can ever do!

As the Master of Zen Shiatsu, Tetsugen Serra, observes: *"the fundamental experience for the human being, regardless of their ethnic origin or social status, is not the verbal communication, but, rather, the direct physical connection." (2)*

When we apply a gentle touch to our body – and some areas are more sensitive than others – we release soothing chemicals such as serotonin, which can help us feel more at ease with ourselves, more balanced internally and more comfortable with our physical and social environment.

I would like you to experience the above by practising the exercise below.

Wear something loose and comfortable, lie down, close your eyes, take a few slow and deep breaths and then, start the following sequence of gentle touches:

> begin with your abdomen; make sure that your hand is warm (you can do that by rubbing your hands together) and place your hand directly on your abdomen; now, slowly and gently rub your abdomen, with a circular motion that has,

as the centre, your navel, with a radius of approx. 1 and ½ inches;

➢ move up to your face; locate your 'third eye', which is a small cavity between your eyes and just above them; using the tip of your finger, rub it, slowly and gently with a circular motion;

➢ place use fingertips on your temples; hold them there, still, for a moment; then begin massaging your temples, slowly and gently, in a circular motion. Please do this very gently, as our temples are a very sensitive part of our system;

➢ place both hands on your mastoids, which are the two conical prominences on our temporal bones, just behind our ears; begin massaging them, gently and slowly, with a circular motion;

➢ place the tip of one of your fingers on one eye-lid and begin rubbing it, very softly, in a circular motion; do the same with the other eye-lid;

➢ place the tip of one of your fingers, from each hand, on either side of your mouth (i.e. the right hand's finger on the right side of your mouth, and likewise for the left. Begin massaging this area, with a synchronic and gentle circular motion;

➢ move down to your chin; place the tip of one of your fingers on it and start massaging it, slowly and gently, with a circular motion;

➢ move down to your abdomen and repeat point a), only now you are, first, massaging it, and, then, you complete the exercise by gently rubbing it a few times, always in a circular motion.

Acknowledgements

A special "thank you" to Margaret Russo, who has helped turn the original manuscript of this work into the current version and to Anette Foss Ball, for her advice on body movements.

Notes

Introduction

1. Servan-Schreiber in Burne (2004)
2. Van der Kolk in Pointon (2004), p. 11

1. Energy

1.   Buddha in Kornfield (1994), p. 47
2.   Nice Guideline No. 23 (2004)

2. Presence

1. Buddha   in   Kornfield (1994), p. 37

3. Light heart

1.   Rossi, V. (2004)
2.   Serra, T. (2005)

Bibliography

Books

Assagioli, R. (1971) *Psychosynthesis*, New York: Viking.

Beck, A. T. (1991) *Cognitive Therapy and the Emotional Disorders*, London: Penguin Books.

Bellino, F. (1988) *Etica della Solidarieta` e Societa` Complessa (Ethics of Solidarity and Complex Society)*, Bari: Levante.

Bettelheim, B. (1982) *Freud and Man's Soul*, London: Penguin Books.

Borrelli, S. E. & Palumbo, T. (2004) *Italy,* in Malley-Morrison K. (ed.)

International Perspectives on Family Violence and Abuse, Mahwah (NJ): Lawrence Erlbaum Associates.

De Crescenzo, L. (1983) *Storia della Filosofia Greca – I Presocratici (History of Greek Philosophy, Part 1)*, Milano: Mondadori.

De Crescenzo, L. (1986) *Storia della Filosofia Greca – Da Socrate in poi (History of Greek Philosophy, Part 2)*, Milano: Mondadori.

De Crescenzo, L. (2002) *Storia della Filosofia Medioevale (History of Medieval Philosophy)*, Milano: Mondadori

Dryden, W. (1999) *Rational Emotive Behavioural Counselling in Action*, London: Sage.

Filippani-Ronconi, P. (1994) *Il Buddismo (Buddhism)*, Roma: Newton Compton.

Freud, A. (1993) *Anna Freud: Her Life and Work*, London: Freud Museum Publications.

Freud, S. (1991) *Introductory Lectures on Psychoanalysis*, London: Penguin Books.

Furedi, F. (2004) *Therapy Culture*, London: Routledge.

Goleman, D. (1995) *Emotional Intelligence*, Glasgow: ThorsonsAudio.

Gross, R. D. (1999) Psychology: *The Science of Mind and Behaviour*, London: Hodder & Stoughton.

Hadot, P. (1999) *Philosophy as a Way of Life*, Oxford: Blackwell.

Hirst, B. (2002) *Il riso non cresce sugli alberi (Rice does not grow on trees)*, Milano: La Tartaruga.

Jacobs, M. (2002) *Psychodynamic Counselling in Action*, London: Sage.

Kornfield, J. (1994) *Buddha's Little Instruction Book*, New York: Bantam Books.

Laszlo, E. (1978) in Bellino, F. (1988) *Etica della Solidarieta` e Societa` Complessa (Ethics of Solidarity and Complex Society)*, Bari: Levante.

Lazarus, A. A. (1997) *Brief but Comprehensive Psychotherapy*, New York: Springer.

Lawrence, J. in *The Bathroom Inspiration Book*, Saddle River (NJ): Red-Letter Press.

Lefever, R. (2003) *Eating Disorders*, Nonington (Kent): Promis.

Lerner, M. D. and Sheldon, R. D. *Acute Traumatic Stress Management*, New York: AAETS.

Petronio, G. (1977) *Italia Letteraria (History of Italian Literature)*, Roma: Palumbo.

Pinel, J. P. J. (2003) *Biopsychology*, Boston: Allyn and Bacon.

Rossi, V. (2004) *La via del movimento*, Diagaro di Cesena: Macroedizioni

Serra, T. (2005) *Zen Shiatsu,* Milano: Fabbri

Smail, D. (1993) *The Origins of Unhappiness*, London: Harper Collins.

Smail, D. (1998) *How To Survive Without Psychotherapy*, London: Constable.

Thich Nhat Hanh (1997) in Luchinger, T. *Steps of Mindfulness (video)*, Zurich: Luchinger.

Vinay, M.P. (1973) *Hygiene Mentale (Mental Hygiene)*, St Francois Sherbrooke: Editions Paulines.

Articles, papers and training

Burne, J. (2004) *Can this man cure your depression?* The Independent Review, 17 May 2004.

Canter, D. (2002) *The rise and rise of biobabble*, New Scientist, Vol. 173, issue 2336, 30 March 2002, p. 50.

Davidson, R. (2004) in Huppert, Baylis, Keverne (2004) *The science of well-being*, The Psychologist, Vol. 17, No. 1, p. 7.

Deary, I. (2003) *Ten Things I hate about Intelligence Research*, The Psychologist, Vol. 16, No 10, p. 537.

Fairburn, C. G. and Harrison P. J. (2003) *Eating Disorders*, Lancet 2003; 361: 407-16.

Farley, P. (2004) *The anatomy of despair*, New Scientist, Vol. 182, issue 2445, 01 May 2004, p. 42.

Healy (1998) in Palumbo, T. (1999) *A brief Introduction to Essential Psychology*, London (unpublished paper).

Lanza del Vasto (1975), poet, Christian mystic and non-violent activist, Fellowship Magazine, Sept. 1975.

Lawson, W. (2004) *The Glee Club*, Psychology Today, February 2004, p. 34.

Malley-Morrison, K. (2004) *The Evil of Inaction*, Talk given to graduating MA students, Boston University, 16 May 2004.

Morelli, R. & Zerbini E. (2006) *Training in Anti-stress Bodywork,* Rome: Riza Institute.

Palumbo, T. (1999) *A brief Introduction to Essential Psychology*, CMQ, Vol. X, No. 2 (286), London: GCD.

Pointon, C. (2004) *The future of trauma work*, Counselling and Psychotherapy Journal UK, May 2004, p. 10.

Rowe, D. (2001) *The story of depression*, Counselling and

Psychotherapy Journal UK,
November 2001, p. 5.

Small, M. F. (2002) *The happy fat*,
New Scientist, Vol. 175, issue 2357,
24 August 2002, p. 34.

Thernstrom, M. (2001) *Life Without
Pain*, The New York Times
Magazine, December 16, 2001, New
York.

Van der Kolk, B. A. (2002) *EMDR,
consciousness and the body*, Boston:
The Trauma Center.

Resources

DesMaisons K. (2001) *Potatoes not Prozac*, London: Simon & Schuster.

Kornfield, J. (1994) *Buddha's Little Instruction Book*, New York: Bantam Books.

Tolle, E. (2005) *The Power of Now,* London: Hodder & Stoughton